THE ENTREPRENEUR FOR A NEW ERA

How the 'awareness-based entrepreneur' becomes the forerunner for the new economy and what you can do to become one.

> *Every day you are part of the history of the future,*
> *often unaware of the role you play in it*
> *until the day you consciously take on that task...*
> *~ Marc Hermans*

© Marc Hermans, 2020
© Current edition, Marc Hermans, 2020
All rights reserved
ISBN: 9798 -600672635

Cover design: BloomTown

Have you ever asked yourself this?   6
Exciting or scary?   7

Why a new era?   9
What is wrong with the 'old' era?   10
What does this mean for entrepreneurs?   13
What does an 'awareness-entrepreneur' do differently?   15
How does the ego work?   17
How is the ego at the core of the current economy?   20
Misleading information about the 'new era'   22

Know thyself   27
Where the real power is   29
The obstacle   32
The solution   34

The New Era   37
Start with why?   38
Phase 1 - Preparing your Self...   42
    ... so you can create the opportunity   42
    ... so you can be consistent   44
    ... so you can make clear decisions in the Now   48
Phase 2 - Changing your ways...   51
    ... knowing your 'why'   51
    ... knowing the ego   55
    ... being your true self   58
    ... knowing the Obstacles   62
Phase 3 - Going beyond...   64
    ... by helping others   64
    ... by choosing life   65

Redefining 'success'   69

Have you ever asked yourself this?

Have you ever asked yourself how we got here? Or maybe how we might change the way we do things and make the world a better place to live in? I have asked myself and investigated these kinds of questions for many decades. While investigating, I encountered numerous ideas that helped evolve my insight, but they never seemed to truly reveal the core of it all. The main reason that it took me so long to find the answers is that I had to go through a major inner shift before I was ready and able to decipher the clues that were there all the time just waiting to be discovered and understood.

To some, the need for a shift may sound strange, but when looking at our modern society, there is a growing concern about the way we are currently dealing with life on earth. With the complexity of it all, it's obviously a huge challenge to avoid becoming overwhelmed by the number of viewpoints, of which the vast majority is still based on the existing paradigm. Even though in most cases, it is offered with the best intentions, it is crystal clear to me now that the current standard is not the right starting point to solve our problems. One of the most important conclusions I had to draw from my investigations is reflected in a quote from Albert Einstein that says: "We cannot solve our problems with the same thinking we used when we created them".

Exciting or scary?

The idea of a paradigm shift will surely scare some people. What they should be much more scared of, however, is not change itself but instead not being able to make the change before it's too late. For you to understand the new era, you will also need to go through a shift if you haven't already. Therefore, this book is not a "10 rules to becoming successful while saving the world" kind of story, as it would be far too superficial an approach to have any true value. So... are you ready to shift gear with me and find out what is new about the era we are approaching?

Why a new era?

The usual reasons that we hear for the changes that have already begun are mostly sociopolitical in nature. The Stanford Social Innovation Review mentions subjects like "global warming, childhood obesity, unfair labour practice, air and water pollution", for example. However useful the new awareness and understanding of these sociopolitical issues may be, they almost entirely ignore the true cause and the core reason for this necessary shift towards a new era.

Unknowingly, they do touch on it briefly and superficially when stating that "corporations have always had a complex relationship with the rest of society", but they fail to grasp the real significance of their statement. Of course, small-time entrepreneurship and big corporations are a world apart. Still, if we ever hope to improve our situation, it is vital to understand the core issue we are dealing with because it affects all levels of business and economy.

What is wrong with the 'old' era?

'Economy' means different things to different people, depending on their social and financial status and circumstances, and they usually go parallel with their political preferences. So let's start with finding some common ground from where we can enter this new era consciously and cooperatively? The original Greek word 'oikonomia' translates into 'household management'. The management of a household is meant to serve all who live in it while leaving the house intact. Of course, if we would find termites eating our house away, we would want to do something about that. Agreed? It turns out that our house or home is called 'earth', that we humans are not the only inhabitants. Sadly, we do look a lot like the termites in this scenario.

With our economy, we are taking over part of the natural ecology that generally maintains the earth's equilibrium, but we are mostly unbalancing it. Without entering into the details, the old economy was more or less acceptable, but only for a situation that no longer exists because our circumstances have changed drastically since then. An obvious reason to want and need a new era is, for example, that we can't wait for breathable oxygen and clean drinking water to become scarce, and then have some corporation or another filter it to sell it to us for an absurdly high price? That is just an extremely ignorant way of managing your 'household', and it will also kill all the non-human inhabitants of our household because they can't buy fresh air and clean water.

Another obvious example is that we are still trying to create jobs because that is what the economy and our (personal) survival demand, even though an enormous amount of what we are producing nowadays is useless, wasteful, and harmful. We could work and produce much less and much more efficiently, while still offering everyone a more than decent living. (Oh wait, we are not offering 'everyone' a decent living yet, even though technically it would be perfectly possible!), but we won't be able to provide everyone with a job in the way the current economy dictates. That is just not practical anymore.

Those are just a few simple examples on an endless list because the reality of it is much more profound and far more embarrassing and urgent than most people care to admit. To make things worse, the emphasis on profit and the need for an income, make it so that the economic paradigm turns us against each other when within a household you're supposed to work together. Within the proper setting, there is nothing wrong with a bit of competition. However, the way in which the current economy is shaped, it either pushes people into survival mode or has them succumb to greediness before taking responsibility for the consequences.

"Making it in whatever field is only meaningful as long as there are thousands or millions of others who don't make it, so you need other human beings to fail so that your life can have meaning."
~ Eckhart Tolle ("A New Earth")

What does this mean for entrepreneurs?

Regardless if we are talking about jobs or entrepreneurship, we will have to face the fact that at some point we cannot keep inventing jobs, products and services for the sake of the economy. We are not supposed to be slaves to the economy. The economy as a system should be helping and supporting us, our society, when it comes to managing our earthly 'household' in the best possible way. To better manage this household, we will need to deepen our understanding of how it all works.

The question we need to answer is this: What is it that makes us intelligent enough to go beyond nature, but yet too clumsy to do it in a non-destructive way? The answer is actually very simple. Our economy is currently completely ego-based, as is practically everything within modern society. Now let's get one thing straight, there is nothing wrong with the ego, and not even with a partially ego-based economy. The ego is necessary and useful, but at this point in history, it does need to evolve and transform, or we won't survive our current shortcomings. We humans will need to move on to the next stage of our evolution if we do not wish to become both slaves and casualties of our own current state. We need to raise our level of consciousness and liberate ourselves from the limitations that block our growth... and yes, it can be done!

At our current level of consciousness, the ego has had at least one crucial effect on humanity for a while, because people needed to individualize and become more personally responsible for their lives. Therefore it is a good sign that now more than ever, younger as well as older generations, and men as well as women have turned towards entrepreneurship and away from steady jobs. This means that people are trying to take their lives into their own hands, even if for some (or many) initially it is kind of forced upon them as a necessary or inevitable step. With increased individualization also comes the inevitable loss of the natural community that guided us. It is the price to pay for individualism, but we have not yet reached the safe haven where we are truly lord and master over our individual inner world. Meaning we are still extremely manipulable and unknowingly programmed by our surroundings and culture, which makes us quite unfree.

In the new era, a special kind of entrepreneurs will lead the way towards an economy that is not solely based on the ego anymore. A big part of the current consciousness level of the ego certainly won't disappear from humanity anytime soon, but right now specific steps can be taken to open the world up to a new kind of economy with a somewhat different focus. Where most big companies still try to figure out the sociopolitical changes that are taking place, this special kind of entrepreneur goes to the core of the shift, which is the change in awareness and self-awareness that humanity is going through right now.

What does an 'awareness-entrepreneur' do differently?

If you want to go straight to the center and source of this change and be(come) an 'awareness-based entrepreneur,' you have to be(come) as aware and conscious as the people you hope to serve and do business with and, preferably, even more conscious then they are. You will need to learn how to transform parts of your ego and overcome other parts of it, and I don't say that lightly. Overcoming the ego is often interpreted as something spiritual, but it is really more of an evolutionary psychological step for humanity. And a necessary step for that matter, because if we get stuck within the ego in the way it is currently functioning in the majority of people, eventually we will encounter nothing but figurative and literal dead ends.

To become more conscious, you should first understand what the ego is and how it works. The term 'ego' as used in this book, applies to 'an accumulation of ideas about yourself that you believe to be true'. This ego offers "a false sense of self" (Eckhart Tolle) that provokes an initial self-awareness, which is part of what separates us from the animals. I mentioned 'false sense of self' and that 'you' have to believe those ideas. Both ways of expressing are not accidental because there is also an actual self or consciousness that can be experienced. It is this real self or consciousness which believes, is emotionally invested in, and gives power to "the story of me" that the ego tells.

Have you ever heard anyone say "I was talking to myself"? Maybe you have used the expression yourself, but what you are actually saying is that you were talking to your 'self' or 'consciousness', either in your mind or out loud. The actual self was there before the ego came into play. When you were a baby, you were already conscious, but not yet self-aware. This initial consciousness is the real self before it becomes semi-self-aware through the ego. Growing up and experiencing life, you learn what kind of 'persona' you believe yourself to be through how you react, and by what the people around you say about you. That persona(lity) slowly turns into a self-fulfilling prophecy because you believe that the ideas in your mind about you are genuine and real. This then translates into numerous behavioral patterns that are stored in the subconscious mind.

Things like "I am shy", "I am an extrovert", "I am always emotional", "I am stubborn", etcetera, are all part of the personality. The word 'persona' not only means "aspect of someone's character". It also describes "a role or character adopted by an author or an actor". The ego contains fragments of truth, but it is not you. Instead, it is (in big part) a role you have taken upon you as a result of a particular disposition in the form of temperament, nature, and constitution, in combination with how you have dealt with past experiences, and how you have been shaped and influenced by your parents, friends and culture. A role that you don't know you are playing, but that does connect with the real you (your self), which makes your 'acting' so convincing.

How does the ego work?

The ego is mind-based, which means it is dualistic by nature (like or dislike, good or bad, right or wrong, etcetera), and its primary focus is on avoiding and escaping discomfort. This focus is not so different from animal instincts, except for the fact that humans are far less pre-programmed with relatively unchangeable reaction-patterns than animals. We can keep on learning more ways to escape discomfort until we die, although it tends to become more challenging to learn new things as we get older.

The main reason it gets more complicated with age is that we learn new things on top of our previously learned and integrated ideas, beliefs and patterns. Within the mind, everything is connected and what we learn (and learn to believe) as small children, form the roots for our later learning (and beliefs).

> *Over the years, your minds activity has grown into your own 'tree' of beliefs and assumptions. Because you identify with the story behind the creation of that 'tree of beliefs' (e.g., your past experiences), you accept it as your self-image. This false but convincing self-image is, in many ways, the dictator and limiter of your current life. It is the filter through which you see and interpret everything, and it even keeps you from enjoying the original sense of freedom with which you were once born.*
> *~ Samwell Newman ("You can be the Guru!")*

This connectedness of all your beliefs, knowledge and learning often makes it extremely difficult to recognize why the ego does what it does. It regularly fools us into believing that our actions are not instinctive, because they are located in the upper levels of Maslow's Hierarchy of Needs, when in fact, the initial roots for things like love and belonging, esteem, and even self-actualization, are usually still our basic needs for safety and survival. That is why the higher levels of the hierarchy are also 'needs' and not yet free choices, as many seem to believe.

Someone who is very meticulous, for example, may have learned as a child that this is a good way to avoid the suffering (i.e., extreme discomfort) that he or she believes will come when making a mistake, but we subscribe it to his or her character. Although there may be certain tendencies in the child that makes it choose this particular way of dealing with situations, the actual motive is its fear of suffering, and this meticulous person likely endured a critical environment when growing up. In other words, it's a coping mechanism.

And what if someone always wants to help others? Surely that is not the ego? Some people find personal pleasure in pleasing others (see "Eckhart Tolle - Desire and Meaning", a fragment taken from "A New Earth"), a trait that can also be learned and adopted at a very early age. The reason for helping still comes from the ego and is aimed at obtaining personal pleasure, so it is not actually about helping others. They escape certain discomforts by doing something that gives them pleasure, which can quickly turn into a habit, and even into an addiction.

> *"Not your aim or your actions are primary, but the state of consciousness out of which they come."*
> *~ Eckhart Tolle ("A New Earth")*

Before you start thinking in terms of good and bad (or evil), it is essential to know that such a judgement is made by the mind, and judging won't get us anywhere but deeper into the mind's dualism. This is not about good or bad. It is about understanding how the ego works and how to rise above its current limitations.

> *"...there is nothing either good or bad,*
> *but thinking makes it so."*
> *~ William Shakespeare*

How is the ego at the core of the current economy?

The current economy has entrepreneurs creating and managing businesses for profit. Could there be a more egotistical goal? Another aspect where the ego is of great importance and easily recognizable is in marketing and advertisement. In connecting products and services to existing beliefs in the ego of a target group, the product or service is made tempting to a potential client. However, many things that are sold this way are not actually interesting, or at least not as important as the ego believes them to be. The illusions within the ego are connected to the illusions that are created and suggested around the products and services that businesses try to sell.

For example, many egos believe that status is important, so certain types of cars are turned into symbols that enhance the standing of the owner. It is all perception and not reality, but that is typically what happens within the ego, and the car industry uses that principle to sell more (expensive) cars. If you compare it to what happens within a group of gorillas, the similarities are frightening. Where the macho uses his muscles, posture, and physical display to impress and subdue the other gorillas, we humans use all kinds of objects, like cars, houses, clothing, jewelry, etcetera to impress and subdue other egos.

It is kind of sad to realize, that even though we are equipped with a mind that is superior to that of a Gorilla, we still often act like them, albeit through the use of advanced toys and egotistical behavior. Of course, that is what happens when we live by the standards of the ego, which grow from the same roots of similar basic instincts that the Gorillas have. Fortunately, the ego as we know it is not the end of it. It's just the beginning.

Misleading information about the 'new era'

The term 'new era' may raise suspicion among some of you, because the term is regularly used for marketing purposes to attract entrepreneurs, based on the idea that we have to stay ahead of the competition, for example. According to young entrepreneur Peter J. Voogd, who also talks about a "new era for business", entrepreneurship "is really not about you". With that, he refers to the people that depend on entrepreneurs, like their families. But family is, in most cases, an extension of the ego so seeing entrepreneurship that way, does not change anything. He also mentions 'hunger to succeed' as a motivator, which connects to what I explained about our instinctive ego-nomical behavior. That becomes even more obvious when he names money as an example of a 'core value' (i.e., the fundamental beliefs of a person or organization).

It raises the question of what a young and reasonably successful entrepreneur like him might see as vital for the new era. In his words, it's about "creating opportunities based off of who you really are". According to Voogd, "the biggest key to success is who you surround yourself with". In the youtube video "The New Era of Entrepreneurship - Peter Voogd Keynote Speech | Mexico |" he explains that "who you surround yourself with is who you become, so you need to evaluate how they are making you feel and think".

This view on "who you really are" is where the mixup starts, because he and so many others still base that completely on the current consciousness level of the ego. However, it bases off a level of consciousness that believes that others can make you feel and think things without your consent and help when, in fact, everything that you experience, you experience inside of you. Even when shaking hands with someone, you don't feel the other persons' skin but instead your own reaction to it from the nerves in your skin. Of course, that is an automated physical reaction that can't be avoided, and it is merely what you feel in your skin and muscles. It is not yet "how it makes you feel", because that part is up to you.

Buddha's story of the two arrows explains how physical pain is inevitable, while mental suffering is optional. In other words, there is no need to become like the people you interact and surround yourself with because they are not the rulers over what you feel and think. You are the ruler, or you can be if you learn how to manage your inner self. The question now becomes: How can you ever hope to base your actions on who you really are, if you mistake your ego for your true self? The answer is, you can't. And that is why we need to know and understand who we really are before we can successfully change the world we live in.

Eckhart Tolle's book "A New Earth" is a fascinating read when trying to understand ourselves and the shift in consciousness that is taking place right now, but many others are dedicating their life and work to this. I have achieved a lot of clarity from the book titled "You can be the Guru!" (by Samwell Newman), for example, because I needed a practical step by step approach that engages the thinking mind as a stepping-stone towards increased consciousness and freedom.

Know thyself

To know yourself, you will need to free your self and consciousness from the modern dictatorship of the mind and the ego. In many ways, that is contrary to what our current society tells and teaches us. Modern culture labels being 'out of your mind' as 'crazy', but crazy means 'mad as manifested in wild or aggressive behavior'. Surprisingly, waking up from the spell of the mind and ego provokes precisely the opposite. It offers inner peace and harmony, which is the only space where true inner freedom can exist. Additionally, "the separation of thinking and awareness" (as Eckhart Tolle describes it in "A New Earth") helps us see more clearly than ever how 'crazy' some of our egoic behavior actually is.

The mind and ego are primarily motivated by discomfort, often in the form of a sense of lack. Over time, this grows into a variety of (compulsive) needs that all stem from the basic root-need to avoid discomfort. The never-ending demand for 'more' that is typical for our current economy matches perfectly with how the modern-day mind and ego function because to the mind and ego, just 'being' is never enough. As an awareness-entrepreneur, appealing to the ego of potential customers is still the primary doorway to getting attention for your product or service amongst prospects. Where you can make a difference, however, is in what kind of need you try to connect to, and in what happens after you connect, which will depend on your motives.

Trying to connect through a more basic need like safety will usually not help you get in contact with people (the side of people) that might be open to a deeper connection, but you can appeal to the needs that are closest to the real self. You will find those needs at the top of the self-actualization needs within Maslow's hierarchy of needs. Some have even added a new top layer to Maslow's pyramid called 'self-transcendence', which would make sense if the so-called self-transcendence grew from egoic roots. However, the actual expansion of consciousness that comes from knowing the real self liberates and transforms the existing egoic layers rather than adding a new one. To understand this better, we also need to understand our true power: The power of 'self'.

Where the real power is

The self is what gives power to your ego to the point where it has shaped your ego into a semi-independent force or 'entity'. Because the real self of most people is heavily invested in their ego, the self can best be reached indirectly through the ego at first, and ever more directly after that. As a pioneer in awareness-entrepreneurship, your own progress also needs to be maintained and expanded, because it is easy to let the ego creep back into your thoughts and actions after a while. The day to day challenges we face often have that effect on us because our egoic reactions are so well automated that they seem natural to us. Practice is needed to not succumb to the 'temptations of the ego' within our fast-moving modern world.

> *"A good intention is not enough. You have to be conscious throughout the creative process."*
> *~ Eckhart Tolle ("A New Earth")*

So the real power is not in the mind or ego but in the self or consciousness. The question is, how do we access it directly without the filter of the ego? Terms like 'self' and 'consciousness' can stir up a lot of questions and tend to create confusion. People ask if it is the soul, if it is situated somewhere in the brain, if it has something to do with the 'higher self', etcetera, but for the intentions of an awareness-entrepreneur, it doesn't matter.

What matters is that it is there, that it can be experienced directly, and that it is far more powerful than most people realize. So powerful, that the direct experience of it could change your life forever. Unfortunately, it can also be difficult to experience the self at first because the mind has been our go-to place for such a long time, and this new experience feels utterly different from anything the mind can produce. On top of that, the entity we call ego will try and 'fight back' whenever it feels threatened and scared by this new experience. It will view much of it as a huge discomfort that needs to be avoided and escaped from immediately.

You already experienced the self (meaning: the state of 'being' that is not like any state of mind) before, but at such a young age that you did not yet have the self-awareness and consciousness that you have today. You still lived entirely in the present moment, and the ego had not been (fully) formed yet. Young children live in the now, as Eckhart Tolle calls it in his book "The Power of Now", and are not planning for, or worrying about the future. Nor are they thinking much about the past, and what they experience in that state of being is not stored as typical memories. Instead, it goes almost directly to the subconscious mind, where a lot of traumatic, satisfying, and repeated experiences will form certain reaction-patterns based on the primal reactions that we humans are born with. They form the subconscious roots for our later, partially conscious 'tree of beliefs' (Samwell Newman, "You can be the Guru!").

By following the indications in books like "The Power of Now", we can go back to a similar state of being in which we are not conditioned by the mind and ego while maintaining our 'adult' self-awareness, knowledge, and insights. In other words, we don't need to go back to being 'witless' infants to achieve this. Not that the mind and ego are bad, but most of their content is initially grown from primal reactions. What being present and aware in the now does, is create a state that is free from (unnecessary) instinctive reactions that the mind and ego automatically (re)produce. That clears the path for another kind of thinking and another level of (self-)awareness.

The obstacle

The main obstacle for awareness-entrepreneurs is also the reason why their success is vital for the process of change that is taking place, and additionally for their success. Entrepreneurs have to provide their own income, and survival instincts and dopamine-based urges are some powerful pushes when it comes to that (hence Peter J. Voogd's views on core values). The problem with that approach, according to Eckhart Tolle, is that the ego's purposes are "relative, unstable, and impermanent", which will eventually lead to unnecessary suffering and inconsistent choice-making, even if we are successful in our endeavors.

When talking about purpose and core values in the way they surge from the ego, they all point toward some "thing". Even if the thing is a physical result and not a mental one, it is always accompanied by an idea and inner belief(s) about that thing, and one or more needs will be coupled with those ideas. The ego regularly goes after external things for an internal reason when it is trying to escape or avoid internal discomfort, even if we are unaware of that fact. When our basic needs and part of our psychological needs are fulfilled, we do move up within Maslow's hierarchy towards the so-called higher needs, but for the ego it will never be 'enough'.

There will always be more discomforts. That means we move between the different levels, depending on our situation and state of mind, but we stay connected to the same primal roots and reactions. For the mind and ego, happiness is practically always out of reach, either in the future or in the past, and hardly ever right here right now for more than a moment or two. Moments of success then need to be repeated over and over again, and every repeated victory will taste a little less sweet than the one before. In this scenario, every next success always has to be bigger and better to satisfy in the same way. That is how success-addictions are created.

The ego has clear addictive tendencies, but an important conclusion can be drawn from identifying the main obstacle: We are continually seeking outside of us that which is inside of us. It has been said many times by gurus and humanities teachers, but those who try to look inside usually encounter a wall called the mind (and ego). More than a wall, it's a filter that colors everything we observe with an accumulation of judgments and beliefs within the mind and ego. The more we apply force from within the mind to get to know and understand our self, the stronger we get trapped inside the mind, and the further we push the self away. When looking at how the mind and ego work, specific patterns become evident. Those patterns consist of a never-ending stream of needs with our basic instincts still at the center of it. We are chasing our tail our whole life, unaware of our true motivations until we learn how to stop this rollercoaster...

The solution

The obvious solution is to rise above our mere instincts, which is done by separating our awareness from our thinking. As long as our consciousness is still fully engaged with and attached to the mind, we are trapped within the boundaries of the mind and ego. As soon as our awareness lets go of (part of) the identification with and attachment to the mind and ego, it is free to experience life directly. From there, the self can also be experienced directly, not as an object but from within as pure awareness.

The 'awareness', 'self', or 'consciousness', that is your true core, who you really are, the power of 'you' (Eckhart Tolle calls it the 'I am') with which you were born. You are not the thoughts in your mind but the observer of those thoughts. You are not the ego, but the one who believes to see itself reflected in the ego. Separate the observer and the thinking mind, and many of your thoughts will immediately lose credibility because, at that moment, your self is no longer maintaining the emotional bond with those thoughts. The source of the power of the ego comes from the emotional attachment your self maintains with the ideas about you in the mind, and not from the thoughts and ideas themselves. That emotional attachment by the self or consciousness turns ideas into beliefs which then grow into an entire belief-system or 'tree of beliefs' (Samwell Newman - "You can be the Guru!").

While the mind and ego are chasing ever-changing goals which all come with an expiry date, the consciousness or self has but one purpose that will not expire anytime soon:

> *"Human beings are meant to evolve into conscious beings [...] Your inner purpose is to awaken. It is as simple as that. You share that purpose with every other person on the planet..."*
> ~ Eckhart Tolle ("A New Earth")

Just think about it for a moment. If the evolutionary step after animal-consciousness is the ego, which works as a mirror for us to learn about ourselves, it clearly points toward this common purpose to "evolve into conscious beings".

The New Era

We have all heard that the power is with the consumer, but even the word 'consumer' hints to the fact that the power is with the extremely unstable and highly manipulable ego. The first contact between businesses and the public is through the ego, so the power is actually with the companies that use and manipulate the ego to their advantage and profit. (Those who are already in the process of liberating themselves from the ego will often become less consumeristic and will have less power within the economy while they form a small minority. Only when enough people have liberated themselves, will their influence become noticeable.)

The New Era can take many forms and shapes, but the main purpose will be to awaken, to become more conscious and aware, instead of being ruled (only) by the mind and ego. It is the one purpose we have in common, even though many people are not yet aware of it. That is precisely why the awareness-based entrepreneurs have such an important role to play in the years to come. But how can we shape and apply that purpose so that it helps us fulfill that role?

Start with why?

Many of you may have seen the TED Talk titled "Start with Why" in which Simon Sinek explains how successful and inspired companies and organizations communicate and act from the 'Why'.

> *"People don't buy what you do.*
> *People buy 'Why' you do it..."*
> ~ Simon Sinek ("Start with Why")

For a while, this TED Talk had a lot of entrepreneurs searching for their 'why', and many found one or two and started to communicate them. Sadly, a lot of them did not get the results that they were hoping for. Truth be said, it can sound quite 'orthopedic' if you have to search for or 'invent' your 'why' because you believe it will help you sell more. Especially now that we know that most people are pretty much unaware of the true origin of their root-motives. Also, merely explaining to the world why you do something, which is how many understood Sinek's TED talk, is not at all the message that he meant to transmit. What went wrong for those unfortunate why-tellers?

As I said earlier, the first contact will still be all about perception from the mind and ego. Apple, Simon Sinek's favorite example of a company that communicates their 'why', spent vast amounts of dollars on masterly crafted campaigns to create the perception of the rebel amongst computer companies. It is true that their philosophy, or at least Steve Job's philosophy, was different from that of their competitors, so they were not just empty words. The perception that they created was based on a core of reality and was recognizable throughout the entire company, as well as in all Apple's products.

At least two clear elements seem to be necessary to make this approach work:

1. The motivation or 'why' has to be genuine and constant within the organization.

2. It has to be offered in a way that resonates with the people the company tries to communicate to and with.

Of course, point number one should not be a surprise to anyone; it has to be authentic and constant, or no one will believe you. (At least not in the long run.) Point number two has to do with the fact that (from an egoic viewpoint), initially, people are not interested in your organization or you. They want to know what you or your organization could mean to them. In other words, which discomfort can you can help them avoid or distract them from. There is, however, another discomfort (read: fear) that humans automatically direct to an unknown entity, namely an initial doubt about your trustworthiness. These kind of questions are asked unconsciously, but they need to be answered: Can you be trusted? Is what you say true?

We also ask ourselves that whenever we meet someone new and what we instinctively look for are things we might have in common or disagree on with the yet unknown person. We may not be aware of it, but in those moments, our survival instincts drive us. Looking for common ground is a tactic that helps us judge the situation. Is it safe to relax and open up, or might this person (or company) be a threat somehow? That is why marketing and advertising aim at creating trust between the company and the (potential) clients. Apple's 'why' was translated into a way of looking at the world that resonates with people, especially the early adopters, so that those people would assume and believe that Apple's products would also resonate with them.

Even though that is the primary use of marketing and advertisement, to make it work for people with more awareness, the stakes are a bit higher. The motives of an awareness-entrepreneur will have to go beyond the ego of the entrepreneur, or it will just be a facade. The ego-based entrepreneurs believe in and can stand behind their ego-based story, which can make them convincing enough for an ego-oriented client. Most ego-based entrepreneurs will find it difficult, though, to be consistent and not come about as promoting his or her self-interest.

Although I used Steve Jobs as an example, I'm not saying that Jobs was an awareness-entrepreneur. Jobs had quite an obsessive personality and some very strong ideas about how things should be, which is one of the reasons the results of his work are slowly fading now that there is no one left within Apple that has the same kind and level of obsessiveness. Jobs personified the why from his ego and could maintain it through obsession while he was the head of Apple, but it turns out to be unsustainable now he is no longer there to obsess over it.

> *"Without living in alignment with your primary purpose, whatever purpose you come up with, even if it is to create heaven on earth, will be of the ego or become destroyed by time. Sooner or later, it will lead to suffering. If you ignore your inner purpose, no matter what you do, even if it looks spiritual, the ego will creep into how you do it, and so the means will corrupt the end."*
> Eckhart Tolle ("A New Earth")

Phase 1 - Preparing your Self...

> *"We could completely redefine ourselves, or we could simply decide to let our real selves shine through."*
> ~ Tony Robbins

... so you can create the opportunity

The awareness-entrepreneur has gone or is going through some personal shifts that have reshaped and will continue to reshape his or her 'why'. A far more profound core purpose and 'why' will surface, namely "the evolution into a conscious being" (Eckhart Tolle - "A New Earth"). Even though you want your clients to choose your products, services, company, or simply you (if you work freelance) over your competition from a place of awareness, you still need to appeal to their more superficial 'why' first, if you want them to listen to you.

You might think that it is possible to get directly through to the consciousness of someone who has gone through a shift that resembles yours, but that is usually not the case. Almost all first contact (even more so online), especially if it is not yet set up in a predefined situation of trust, will go through the filters of the mind and ego first. For example, a Facebook group about a specific subject would be a situation of trust for those who want to discuss that topic, but not for them to trust you as an entrepreneur who is trying to get attention for his or her product or service. In such a group, the people usually do not want or expect to be bothered with 'take a look at what I have to offer' kind of posts and actions that go against what the group was created for, so their defenses typically go up when they are confronted with them.

We all know that trust needs to be earned, but you will first have to create the *opportunity* before you can even start earning it. To do that, you have to pass through the filter of the minds and egos, even in the case of more conscious and aware people. An obvious but important reason why the point of entry still needs to be the ego is that, in our time, people have to deal with an absolute overload of information, offers, and stimuli. The good news is that the minds and egos of more aware people are prepared or 'trained' to recognize, understand, and receive awareness-orientated messages in the language of the ego. Their minds are open to that specific range of frequencies when other people will either overlook or reject them.

However, before you can even think about ways to create opportunities, you need to make sure that you are conscious and aware enough yourself to apply it in a manner that connects to the right frequency. As an aspiring awareness-entrepreneur, your first focus is to become increasingly aware of what might be keeping you from being an effective awareness-entrepreneur. You can only be authentic and constant if you are not an easy victim to the unstable tendencies within your own mind and ego, and the external influences that sway them.

... so you can be consistent

In phase one, awareness-entrepreneurs will focus on the personal shift towards increased presence and awareness by being present and aware in the now as often and as long as they can. In that state of 'being', the world looks very different from when the filter of the mind and ego are activated. It is in those moments that new ways of entrepreneurship and creativity can enter our awareness, but don't try to use it for that. When trying to be present and aware to achieve a specific goal, presence, and awareness will elude you, and the mind will take charge again. The mind and ego focus on an outcome or result when the focus should be on presence and awareness.

This is the reason that so many entrepreneurs get stuck in the limbo of phase one and unknowingly fall back into the mind and ego every time. Phase one is full of traps, and because it is so different from what we are used to, we often only recognize after a while that we have lost our consciousness to the mind and ego again. I advise all aspiring awareness-entrepreneurs to read (or listen to the audio)book of Eckhart Tolle's "Power of Now". There are also numerous videos on YouTube in which he explains how to deal with specific egoic tendencies and patterns. Identify your most significant weak point(s) when it comes to your ego, and search for videos that help you with that.

The purpose of stage one is sustained consciousness and awareness, self-knowledge, and self-awareness that goes beyond the ego. The wall we need to take down is within us, so we need to understand that wall and start taking it down wherever and whenever we can. Every brick we take out of that wall will offer us a better view of what the new era encompasses. And for those who haven't noticed, the current 'battle' is fought over the mind through manipulation of the mind and ego.

Because of the explosion of media-technology in our time, the different media are now competing for our ego's attention and tear us apart with countless distractions nearly every minute of our waking life. We want to learn how to be and stay in control of our focus and attention. That starts with consciousness, presence, awareness, with being in the now, with being able to leave the mind alone, and learning to know and understand the workings of the ego. For example, the ego is highly influenced by our culture, and within our culture, modern science has profoundly changed our way of thinking and looking at the world, but...

> *"Science will proof to you anything but the meaning. From science you will only get what it is made of."*
> ~ Allan Pittman

When talking about the *essence* or what is *essential*, you are talking about what something 'is' (Latin: *essentia* and *Esse*, which means 'be'). In the case of the human 'being', science can cut a human open and tell us what we are made of, and that is very useful. But it is unable to understand the 'being' part of it. Science is, therefore, unable to explain life and consciousness. What is strange about that, is not necessarily science's inability to tell us what they are, but the fact that so many people are truly convinced that science does explain, and has already revealed what life and consciousness are. This clearly shows how poorly we are using such an essential feature as our thinking, and how easily we are fooled by the marvels of scientific discovery (partially because of how science is 'marketed', by the way).

We can easily understand this phenomenon once we realize that our thinking is not yet our own. Instead, we inherit its current functioning from our culture, our family, our education, and how it is managed and manipulated by and through the media. Furthermore, the speed with which new information and distractions reach us makes it near to impossible to deepen our insights. Still, we are searching for it, hungering for it even. Hence the widespread love of profound quotes that are often not understood in the way they were meant, because the context is missing and few have found the time and opportunity to read the entire texts from which they were extracted. Deep down, we want to know, but people's actions are often still little more than lazy attempts from the mind and ego to achieve a pleasant state of mind with it.

To avoid getting stuck there ourselves, the preparation and training in presence and awareness that Eckhart Tolle describes are vital for our success as an awareness-entrepreneurs. We cannot be consistent if we are still a slave of our current compulsive mind and ego. The daily challenges and distractions are too much and too strong to walk a straight path with just the mind and ego as our guide.

How many of you have fallen for the 'free seminar' offers and have even considered offering one yourself? At first, I believed that there could be a small percentage that actually might be useful, consistent, or at least honest about there intentions, instead of just being a cloaked sales pitch and a waste of time. After having checked out thirty or so different seminars, I gave up. Their intentions are usually too obvious, and not one of them left me with something I could use. Some were quite good at manipulating the mind and ego, though. So good that, for a moment, I even considered some of their offers. Until I realized that I had lost my presence and awareness, but as soon as I woke up from the spell I had been under, the offers seemed largely nonsensical to me.

... so you can make clear decisions in the Now

It is not just the distractions and manipulation that takes us away from awareness. Even the planning we do can be an awareness-killer. Planning is necessary, but we tend to overdo it because of how the mind and ego seek to control our future. Awareness-entrepreneurs only plan what actually needs planning, and they avoid turning it into a habit to plan. Projecting ideas toward the future and then getting attached to those plans and ideas, especially when the mind turns them into (fantasized) success-stories, are typical for the mind and ego. Instead, you will want to choose a direction based on a purpose. That way, the end-result does not depend on a fixed form or path, and you can leave space for your learning curve, coincidence and synchronicity, and the unexpected. Believing that by projecting forms into the future, we get the best result is not only outdated and has been proven wrong in every aspect of life, it is also based on what the mind and ego want, which makes it food for inconsistent behavior and choices.

Of course, the opposite can also happen when we see nothing but bears on the road. This mind-trick that is typically activated out of fear of future suffering. The way to avoid it is by regularly observing the mind, the ego, and your emotions. Try and understand how, when, and why negative thoughts about the future, a 'need' for planning, and fantasies about future success or failure are triggered. To help you see through those tendencies, it is crucial to understand that the unobserved mind and ego focus on one single thing, namely to avoid any discomfort. To achieve that, the system will often present you with some fear (worries) to warn you for the possibility of future suffering. There are the more obvious pictures it paints in your imagination, like poverty, hardship, and other kinds of evident distress. Still, it can also be something as simple as the fear of missing out on an opportunity, or shame, ridicule, failure, etcetera.

Another way in which the mind and ego try to avoid discomfort is by escaping it with something that gives pleasure. Those pleasures can quickly turn into addictions when the subconscious mind saves them as automated reaction-patterns for certain situations and specific types of discomfort. As I mentioned before, the ego may also hang a carrot before you like 'happiness and pleasure that awaits you in the future'. Things like success and money, but also freedom and safety. Al these patterns are used to avoid discomfort, but they take you away from experiencing the Now. By increasing your consciousness and awareness about the specifics of these reactions, you can purge them little by little.

But don't get ahead of yourself. At first, let it happen and let your mind and ego do their thing while you observe them from a state of presence and awareness. Learn from them, become conscious of them, and don't judge them(!). Maybe you could also take some time at the end of the day to look back and see what kind of unconscious reactions and patterns emerged within the mind and ego? Recognizing them is the key to turning them into triggers of awareness. Once you get to know the movements of your mind and ego, your awareness will get a little boost every time there is such an automated reaction that needs your conscious attention. Until now, those reactions would have come out naturally and unguarded, but with your new awareness, you get the chance to do something else and make a conscious decision in the Now.

Phase 2 - Changing your ways...

... knowing your 'why'

We saw earlier that there are two major elements to making the 'why' effective:

1. The motivation or 'why' has to be genuine and constant within the organization.

2. It has to be offered in a way that resonates with the people the company tries to communicate to.

To make this happen without being obsessive about it, there's a third element that came from a quote by Eckhart Tolle:

> "Human beings are meant to evolve into conscious beings [...] Your inner purpose is to awaken. It is as simple as that. You share that purpose with every other person on the planet..."
> ~ Eckhart Tolle ("A New Earth")

This is the secret to the awareness-entrepreneurs' 'why' compared to Steve Jobs' obsessive 'why' for Apple. When Simon Sinek talks about the 'why', he explains it as something you deeply believe in and feel so passionate about that you would probably do it for free if you didn't need the money. Of course, what he is talking about, arises from the pleasure-seeking part of the entrepreneurs' ego, so it will not work long term unless it turns into an obsession, and it will definitely not work for the awareness-entrepreneur. (See more about why passion does not work in the TedTalk by Benjamin Todd titled "To find work you love, don't follow your passion").

For many entrepreneurs, the money they earn is their 'why', either because without it, they would soon reach a level of starvation, or at least get into serious financial trouble, or because that is what they are passionate about. Patrick Bet David explains that the 'why' tends to evolve from this elementary level to something beyond the need or love for money. He states that everyone's 'why' goes through four phases, of which 'survival' is the first phase, followed by 'status', and then 'freedom'. He adds a fourth phase he calls 'purpose'. There is an obvious parallel with Maslow's Pyramid of Needs, but it also gives an insight into how your 'why' (or purpose) could align with the minds and egos of the people that you want to help with your product(s) or service(s).

Simon Sinek puts the entrepreneur's level of consciousness at the same height as the ego-focussed passions of their clients, but awareness-entrepreneurs need to be able to understand and see through that ego-consciousness while working from a higher level of consciousness and awareness themselves. That is what the preparation-phase is for. Only when you find a minimum level of freedom from your mind and ego, can you hope to stay consistent, genuine, ánd connect your 'why' or purpose to the passions of people you (wish to) communicate with or to.

If your purpose were confined within the walls of the four phases that Patrick Bet David describes, you would not be able to stay genuine and consistent without being obsessive about it, or out of fear of losing what you have. If, however, you know that "your inner purpose is to awaken and to evolve into a conscious being" (Eckhart Tolle), and that you share this purpose with everyone else, it applies to your whole life and not just to your company. It then becomes your choice to either let your self be steered and directed by your (unconsciously) conditioned mind and ego, or instead to let your inspiration come from the unconditioned oneness and will of your free self and consciousness.

> *"We could completely redefine ourselves, or we could simply decide to let our real selves shine through."*
> ~ Tony Robbins

The difference between the mind and ego, and the self or consciousness, is that the latter is not directly manipulable. Your consciousness can only be manipulated through your mind and ego, and separating thinking and awareness is equal to liberating your self from that manipulation. Of course, that does not happen overnight, nor will the self be freed all at once. Fortunately, life has a way of showing us exactly in which area we need to grow (i.e., become more conscious), and not always in a nice and pleasant way, although that unpleasantness is (in most cases) of our own mind's and ego's making). Still, if you are committed to the task of becoming an ever more conscious being, life will also present you with the fruits of your progress and answers to your questions. Potentially everything is always there already, even if we are yet unable to recognize it. It often 'simply' takes more consciousness to become aware of it, as represented in the well-known saying, 'seek, and you shall find'.

... knowing the ego

The better you understand the working and limitations of the mind and ego, the easier it becomes to see and break through their barriers within yourself, and in others that might be interested in what you have to offer. After some time and practice, you can learn to see the purpose or 'why' behind peoples' actions and words. A purpose that originates from the lower needs within the Maslow's Pyramid of Needs feels different from the ones that come from the higher needs in the pyramid. However, all higher needs still connect to the roots in the lower needs, so it is also very illuminating to become aware of those roots before you act or communicate. The awareness-entrepreneur can make tremendous progress by becoming something of an expert on the working of the ego.

Once your inner purpose has become the inspiration for your actions, and you understand the connection of this purpose with the ego-based translation of it, you are ready to inspire others with what you or your company has to offer. You have switched from reactive to active behavior. When you keep aligning with reality, instead of aligning with the distorted version that your mind and ego previously painted for you, reality will also align more and more with you. That sounds too obvious and like playing with words, but what that encompasses should not be described, because that would make it a mental picture that may or may not be accurate. Just let reality reveal itself to you, and when it does, trust in your presence and awareness to deal with it.

Aligned with reality, things tend to flow, and synchronicities may occur. That is something to be aware of as well, as the ego will try and take hold of that flow and turn it into something it wants to preserve and keep for the future. Alternatively, it may try to turn your attention to the fear of losing the flow. Should the ego succeed, then it will take away your presence and awareness, and the flow will also be gone. Only repeated and prolonged presence and awareness can achieve continuous flow, but not as a goal. Goals are for the mind and ego. You can use them, of course, but only if you do not attach your self to the outcome. Once you start believing that you need a specific result, you have attached your self to it (through the ego), and you are no longer in the Now to experience life and fulfill your purpose of becoming more conscious.

> *"Those who are exceptionally good at what they do may be completely or largely free of ego while performing their work. They may not know it, but their work has become a spiritual practice. Most of them are present while they do their work and fall back into relative unconsciousness in their private life."*
> ~ Eckhart Tolle ("A New Earth")

Knowing your ego means knowing the consequences of your past unconsciousness, including many socially accepted unconsciousness like your personal 'pursuit for happiness'. The pursuit of something is a typically ego-based endeavor, and especially the North-American culture is saturated with it. That kind of realization can hurt (the ego) sometimes because you are emotionally attached to some of them as if they were you. The ego defends itself against increased consciousness and awareness that goes beyond its comprehension. It is the attachment to the story we tell ourselves and others about ourselves that makes the ego. Attachment means that I (my 'self') believes that story to be 'me'. I am like this or like that. Even something like "I am an entrepreneur" is part of that, because we become emotionally attached to that idea as well, but ultimately it is all fiction. Were you an entrepreneur when you were born? No, you were not. What you are is consciousness, and your path through life may direct you towards entrepreneurship. That does not mean you ever really 'are' an entrepreneur.

The mind and ego love putting labels on everything, but for our consciousness and awareness, it is essential to see the difference between when the ego says 'I am' or when the self or consciousness pronounces those words. To be clear, I only use the label 'self' or 'consciousness' so that our minds don't go crazy when we talk about it, but when it is not under the spell of the ego, the self simply 'is'. Everything else is merely a kind of accumulation of labeled concepts that the mind and ego pile up to make sense of it within their limited reality.

... being your true self

Awareness-entrepreneurs are not always too happy about having to sell and market. Selling and marketing have a bad reputation because most people know them as acts of persuasion. It can make them feel manipulative and deceptive, but they try to do it anyway because they need the income, just like their competition. When you become more conscious and aware, you will find that there is often an alternative available, or that you can invent one for your specific situation. Most rules of marketing still apply, because you talk to the ego as a starting point, but some rules and applications you can revise and change to your liking so that you can be your true self as an awareness-entrepreneur. Let's take a look at some easy examples to get an idea of what I am talking about.

I mentioned webinars before. They form part of the idea of giving before receiving, but most use it with receiving as the primary goal in mind. The awareness-entrepreneur may want to approach it differently because authenticity is vital. For example, if you offer something for free, it has to be something you would wish to give, even if it weren't bringing in any new clients. It also has to be something the receivers actually want and can use to their advantage somehow, or it would be nothing but an empty gesture.

Additionally, from the start, you can be very clear with the participants about your intentions, saying that it is a free webinar, but that you would very much appreciate it if they gave you the chance to get to know you, your company, and your products and services. In fact, not explaining that is nothing less an insult to the intelligence of your audience. Do you believe that they won't find out, or at least wonder why you are offering a free webinar? Many already follow part of these indications, but there is always at least one of them missing because their mind and ego get in the way of doing it right.

To leave the choice with the participants if they are willing to know you better, the information about the company should be at the end of the webinar, of course, but with the webinar itself, you are already showing what you are made of. The good thing is that if your webinar is worth their while, you will also stick out above the average webinar, and you will have created even more goodwill amongst the attendees. Another good thing about this approach is that the ones that do listen to you till the end are actually interested. Many who offer webinars, promise a discount or present if they follow the webinar to the end because it will give them more time to persuade the audience that they should buy. Those are ego-based persuasions that will not endure, nor are they creating any actual trust.

A vital part of creating trust is that you are always transparent and honest about your intentions and that you are conscious of the true meaning of your words. I see many entrepreneurs that supposedly offer downloadable ebooks and alike for free, but then they ask for your name and email address and send you an email with the link. Your name and email address is are not only of value to the entrepreneur or company that offers the 'free' ebook, but people, in fact, 'pay' with a bit of personal information and part of their privacy. The term 'free' is used as 'no money involved', but money is not the only thing of (virtual) value there is. The awareness-entrepreneur will try to avoid such ambiguous communication and be open about his or her intentions. He or she will want to search for an alternative course of action (we are, after all, the pioneers of a new era) that is ultimately more beneficial because with it, we build relationships based on honesty and trust.

When offering a free ebook, for example, there is no need to gather emails from people that do not want to be on your mailing list in the hope that pestering them with offers and marketing-talk will ultimately persuade them to buy. A better way for the awareness-entrepreneur is to be transparent, open, and honest, and leave the choice to them. For example, you could start with a (short) introduction in the ebook in which you explain why you are giving away this ebook and that you have added some additional information throughout the ebook that helps them to get to know you (or your organization) better.

There is also more than enough opportunity to invite them somewhere inside the ebook to add their email to your mailing list (if that is interesting for you and the person subscribing), instead of tricking them into giving their information as payment for a 'free' ebook. Leaving the choice to them works better because they already know something about you, and they choose to be added to your list. This means they are interested, and you don't have to work their ego continuously to persuade them. Many of the 'tricked' will unsubscribe as soon as possible. A large percentage of the ones that don't unsubscribe immediately will most likely not even open any of your emails unless you also try to trick them with seductive and manipulative titles and texts that arouse their ego.

Every choice we make as an entrepreneur reflects who we are and what we stand for. Empty words that are not backed up by acts that show they are true can become the preparation of our downfall. We don't want that, and as we've seen in these examples, there is no need to (always) follow the road everyone walks, especially when we become aware that it does not represent our real self. Our choices as awareness-entrepreneurs will pave the way for a new era, and we want to make it a solid road that also assures future opportunities for more improvements and alternative methods of doing things.

... knowing the Obstacles

When choosing to become a pioneer, one of the obstacles is the fact that there is often not a clear path to follow. Therefore much depends on our ability to make effective choices. Making choices is an art on itself, and though it helps a lot to have a clear purpose (the 'why') and consciousness, it is still a process that cannot be done hastily or skipped without suffering the consequences afterwards. The pioneers of awareness-entrepreneurship are learning while developing alternative ways to do business, the pressure is often high, and the temptation to fall back into old habits even higher.

Probably the biggest obstacle of all is the inner world of the entrepreneur because that is where the groundbreaking choices and decisions are made. That is why I dedicate a lot of my time with BloomTown (bloomtown-coaching.com) to helping awareness-entrepreneurs with their decision-making so that their success won't be unnecessarily stagnated because they are (yet) unable to make essential choices. Those are often also the moments that the awareness-entrepreneur might be seduced by the mind and ego to look for a safe haven or choose an easier way out. That would be a shame after all the work that they put in before encountering this obstacle, so it is vital to pass those tests of awareness. Fortunately, there is always the promise that something can be learned from the challenge.

(If you want more information on how BloomTown helps awareness-entrepreneurs find their way, go to https://www.bloomtown-coaching.com or send an email to marc@bloomtown-coaching.com.)

Phase 3 - Going beyond...

... by helping others

A significant change that will take place when the awareness-entrepreneur begins to flourish is that he or she learns to walk ahead of the curve. As advantageous as that may sound, it is the ego that sees an advantage in that kind of situation because it makes the ego feel safe, relevant, invincible even. However, for the true awareness-entrepreneurs, it will have a different meaning because they are much less driven by escaping discomfort and acting from self-preservation.

Helping others does not necessarily mean that you start showing other entrepreneurs how to be(come) an awareness-entrepreneur, although that is a possibility, of course, but rather helping people that you come in contact with in their evolution towards conscious beings. That can take different forms, many of which are yet to be discovered. The awareness-entrepreneur will not only be interested in his or her own consciousness and awareness, but also in the common purpose he or she shares with other people. Which form the help takes that you will offer is for you to decide, but the moment will come if you choose to follow the path of the awareness-entrepreneur.

... by choosing life

You might think that choosing' life' is a far too obvious choice to be mentioned and that even self-preservation is pro-life, but that is only true for animals. History shows that when it comes to human beings, the ego can take the forces of self-preservation to the level of unimaginable damage and destruction. It doesn't matter if global warming is actually happening and if humans have caused it or not. Anyone who can see beyond a rather futile discussion like that knows that we are polluting, endangering, and destroying life on this beautiful planet. It does not take a genius to figure that one out, but the question is: How do we change it?

Increased awareness and consciousness will play an important role. However, this awareness may come too late for some things to be saved from our current destructive ways. Animal and plant species are already dying out, and this is most likely just the beginning. By giving example, the awareness-entrepreneur can show others how we can choose a different path. A path that many might still consider impossible until they see others walk it. If it is within your possibilities and consciousness to do so, the awareness-entrepreneur should always choose life. Using new and more natural materials than plastic, no animal testing, using natural ingredients, taking ecological responsibility, healthy products, treating employees with awareness and dignity, etcetera. All these and more choices will not only make your company future-proof, but it is also an example for others that has the power to increase their level of awareness. It even has the potential to redefine 'success'.

Redefining 'success'

Another thing that will inevitably come on your path when you walk this road is that you will start to redefine what 'success' means to you and in general. From the moment you start preparing yourself by becoming more conscious and aware, your way of looking at entrepreneurship (and at the world) will change. When it comes to success, you may even want to periodically review where you stand because that will unquestionably help you get more clarity. Clarity is essential when it comes to decision-making if we wish to avoid being sucked back into our old ways.

We can experience success only inside of us, just like everything else we experience. Sure, there may be external appreciation and admiration, for example, but that will only feel as success inside of you if you believe that it is what success looks like. If you do see external recognition as success, then you have attached yourself to that idea, and you will always need to find it externally to be able to feel it (again). In other words, you become dependent on the external appreciation to experience success and have become a slave of it. At that point, you are an addict, and that happens to quite a few entrepreneurs.

As we have seen, the opposite road leads to increased consciousness and true freedom. Freedom at the level of the ego merely means being able to do whatever you want whenever you want it. But because it functions at the level of the ego, it is also never enough. Ego's version of freedom is a stepping stone that takes us beyond the animals. Animals are slaves of a limited and mostly preprogrammed skill-set, while we, humans, have quite the Swiss army knife because of our mind's possibilities. Even so, we are still slaves of our unconscious drive to move away from discomfort (with our basic instincts as the roots). To become truly free, we will need to liberate ourselves from those limiting and sometimes destructive forces with presence and awareness. Our success, consciousness, and freedom go hand in hand. Any separation of these three will always be a surrogate of the real thing.

In a small but very revealing book titled "The Will to be Free", Valentin Wember uses the "Moabit Sonnets" to illustrate the true nature of freedom. It shows how even an incarcerated person could feel more free than many who are not literally imprisoned. The author of the "Moabit Sonnets", Albrecht Haushofer, was a prisoner of Hitler's Third Reich during the Second World War. Valentin Wember summarizes the content like this:

> *"Haushofer's understanding, evolved during his incarceration, is this. The reason I am not free is not primarily due to the fact that I have been brutally imprisoned. I am in bondage because my soul is in the clutches of invisible, fettering principles which keep it from soaring freely. The bonds that enchain the soul are automatic reflexes, passions, drives and other instinctive patterns of behavior."*

Haushofer even tributes his newfound freedom to his imprisonment and suffering.

> "[...] I am free, more free than e'er I've been
> I owe it to my body's chained and shackled state."
> ~ Albrecht Haushofer

Wember then goes on to say that "Contemplation, reflection, and thinking are tools that can lift us out of the pit of having forgotten ourselves". Contemplation, reflection, and thinking can indeed do that, but only when they are free of instinctive impulses. Unfortunately, our modern culture does not yet provide us with an education that helps us achieve it, so we need to self-education for that. In time, our culture will adapt to our increased consciousness, but for now, it is in our hands to create and promote the change and shift by means of our personal development. Earlier I mentioned the United States Declaration of Independence, in which the phrase "the pursuit of happiness" is just the last part that goes accompanied by "Life" and "Liberty".

> "[...]We hold these truths to be self-evident, that all men are created equal, that they are endowed by their Creator with certain unalienable Rights, that among these are **Life, Liberty and the pursuit of Happiness**."
> (Taken from the U.S. Declaration of Independence)

"Life, Liberty and the Pursuit of Happiness" sounds a lot like what I said about 'choosing life' and that success, consciousness, and freedom go hand in hand. However, the level of awareness from which these terms are viewed makes a world of difference. Seen from the level of the ego it may look like we are talking about the same thing, but when we rise above the ego, everything gets a different meaning. "Life" is no longer just our life, and not just human life either, but rather life in general wherever it is found. "Liberty" becomes an inner activity, instead of outer freedom. "The pursuit of Happiness" loses the projection towards the future and turns into joy in the present moment. And that is why the awareness-entrepreneur needs to redefine the meaning of success.

> *"If you are concerned about the world, the first thing you need to do is transform yourself into a joyful being. [...] To be successful, one needs insight, inspiration, and integrity."*
> ~ Sadhguru

Redefining success is part of a more significant shift in which every one of us becomes an inventor of the New Era we are moving towards. We can use insights from others like you are doing now by reading this book, but that is just the beginning. True freedom also means, discovery, creation, and invention. There is a need for new ideas and ways of doing and seeing things, but the time of great leaders showing us the road is partially over for those who have passed the threshold of the ego-consciousness.

> *"Every action you perform is a contribution to some aspect of this world. Being conscious of that should keep you inspired."*
> *~ Sadhguru*

We have gone through a phase of intense individualization, and now it is time to integrate with our increased consciousness and awareness all that has been separated by the ego. To make sure that this change also means progress, it is vital not to lose what we have gained, meaning our individuality. The need for leaders is an unconscious need that is based on fear and lack, but we have all we need to liberate ourselves. The only thing missing is the level of consciousness with which to overcome our fears and often petty egoic needs. Experiencing that level of awareness and living your life from that state of being will be your greatest success as a human being and as an awareness-entrepreneur.

> *"It is never too late to be who you might have been."*
> *~ George Elliot*

www.ingramcontent.com/pod-product-compliance
Lightning Source LLC
Chambersburg PA
CBHW050256220526
45465CB00002B/700